Meditations
and Mandalas

Meditations and Mandalas

SIMPLE SONGS

FOR THE

SPIRITUAL LIFE

Nan C. Merrill

CONTINUUM • NEW YORK

1999

The Continuum Publishing Company
370 Lexington Avenue, New York, N.Y. 10017

Copyright © 1999 by Nan C. Merrill

Printed in the United States of America

Library of Congress Cataloging-in-Publication Data

Merrill, Nan C.
Meditations and mandalas :
simple songs for the spiritual life / Nan C. Merrill.
p.   cm.
ISBN 0–8264–1151–7 (alk. paper)
1. Prayers.   2. Mandala.   I. Title.
BL560.M475   1999
291.4'32—dc21   99-48950
CIP

*Dedicated to the
children of the new millennium.
May we all dedicate ourselves
to the renewal
and divinization of planet Earth,
blue-green jewel
afloat in the universal sea.*

Preface

$\mathscr{L}$ife sometimes seems unfair, overwhelming, and confusing, yet is ever balanced by times of joy, peace, assurance, and celebration. Strangely, we *need* this conflict, this wrestling within ourselves and outwardly with others: the grist by which we develop the "pearl of great price"—our own unique wholeness and holiness. *Meditations and Mandalas: Simple Songs for the Spiritual Life* reflects momentary glimpses of this paradox: the terrible loneliness and fear of separation along with the hope, the glorious joy, and the great peace experienced as we come to know the Beloved Friend, Divine Guest, Loving Companion Presence, Holy Wisdom, Divine Mystery—by whatever name—ever with and within us.

Each meditation and mandala is an invitation to reflect prayerfully—aloud or in silence—on its meaning in one's own life. Keeping a daily journal can deepen any insights that emerge and will become a record of some of the ways the Spirit is working in and through one's life . . . signposts along the Sacred Path we travel to discover who we are, Whose we are.

The mandalas illustrating this book emerged as daily meditations over a summer season. This motif, symbolizing wholeness, reconciliation with the opposites, restoration of balance and harmony, enhances the potential for centering us and deepening our times of prayer. These handcrafted mandalas represent the fruits of my own centering prayer and are offered as another dimension to meditation: to be reflected upon with the heart's eye rather than analyzed with the mind.

Perhaps some will be inspired to create their own meditations and mandalas as a way in and through prayer. Whether prayed individually or communally, *Meditations and Mandalas* can be like windows to the soul that awaken inner vistas and open new horizons.

Inspired by the hope for a more peaceful world for the children and grandchildren of the twenty-first century, I pray that this gift of love will bless all generations.

Meditations
and Mandalas

$\mathcal{B}$lessed are you
  who walk with goodness,
  who stand for the right,
  who live in truth.
For you come to know the Friend
  who dwells in the secret room
   of your heart.
You are like an acorn planted
   in fertile soil
  that grows into a mighty oak.
Your life blesses others,
   you radiate love;
  joy delights your heart.

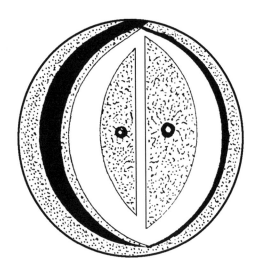

$\mathcal{W}$hy do I set myself apart from the
       Heart of my heart,
   the One Who loves me forever?
Why do I feel unworthy, that I do not
       deserve love—
   as if I am unlovable?
Feeling alone, rejected and forgotten,
   I strike out at others trying
       to prove my worth; or,
   like the turtle, I crawl into my
      shell to hide.

"O dear one, you need never feel
       abandoned,
   or have need to prove your worth.
If you would but pause, be very still,
   and listen to your heart's ear,
       you would come to know that
You are loved by the Friend even more
   than a parent for its child."

You belong to love. Turn not away from
       your true home;
   Make friends with the Beloved of
      your heart!
   Know the joy of sharing that love!

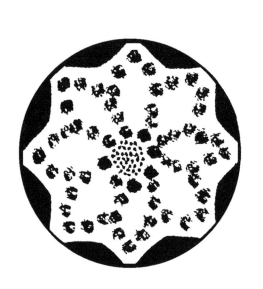

O Friend of my heart, where do my
        fears come from,
    fears that arise in the night
        awakening doubts?
When dreams cause me to tremble,
    I call out to You and within
        my heart You answer:

"Be still, dear one, for all is well.
    Your fears will soon fade away;
    do you not know that love is
        stronger than fear?
Remember, I am with you always,
    closer than your every breath.
        We belong to one another."

Welcome are You, O Divine Friend, in
    the secret room of my heart!

$\mathcal{A}$nswer me, O Friend, when I call!
  Enfold me in the energy of
      your love.
Like a wee babe blanketed in its
      mother's arms,
    let me feel secure and at peace.
Blessed are You, Who hear our prayers,
      our cries in the night,
    and lovingly tend us when we call!

O my Friend, my heart is sad;
    I feel so alone and guilty.
Those who love me are angry—for,
     my words and actions have caused
      much trouble.
How can I face my family and friends?
    How can I make amends?
Walk beside me, O Mender of all
     hearts;
    give me kind words as I
     ask forgiveness,
    help me find ways to repair my
     willful deeds.
You know my sorrow and regret;
    You love me.
 With You, O Faithful Friend, I can
    face my fears;
   I can make amends.

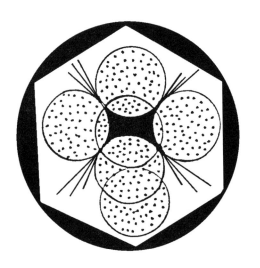

$\mathcal{W}$ill I ever come to know myself when
    I feel like such a stranger?
        Am I worth the effort?
Unkind words spew from my mouth to
        family and friends alike;
    how can this be, when in my heart
        I care for them?
Will I be happy by separating myself
        from those who love me?
Sometimes, I even turn away from You,
    my Friend.

Yet You do not leave me alone with
        my anger and fears;
    You patiently await my call.
When I calm down and listen in silence,
    your voice breaks through my walls:

    "Rest in My love; be not afraid!
Do not let pride keep you from making
        amends with
    those you have hurt by word or
        deed, for
    therein lies healing and freedom.
You are a beautiful child of the universe;
        your birthright is love.
    Be gentle with yourself and learn
    each time you forget your true self.
        Know that I am with you always."

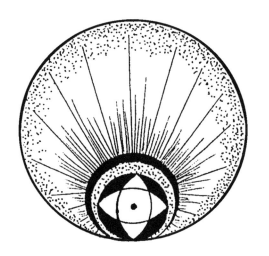

$\mathcal{H}$ave you not heard, do you not know,
the One Who loves you with an
eternal love
is the ever-present Friend, Who
abides in your heart!
Close as your very breath, the Healer
of broken hearts
awaits the call from those who pray
for forgiveness and healing,
those who are ready to make amends.

Joy and a blessed inner peace come
when burdens of guilt, jealousy,
and anger,
all that keeps you separated
from love, are forgiven.
The Heart of your heart is kind and gracious,
quick to forgive and eager for you
to share in the great
dance of life!

$\mathcal{L}$et us sing to the Creator of the cosmos,
       to the divine power of love!
When we look at the wondrous display
       of the heavens,
    at the Earth with its infinite
       variety of life,
Who are we that You love us, that You
       rejoice in our being;
    that You trust us to care for creation
       in all its splendor,
    inviting us to become co-creators
       with You?
Let us celebrate the mystery of life!
    Let us commit our lives to
       the Divine Plan!

$\mathcal{B}$lessed are you who face your fears, and
    who have the courage to walk
        through them;
    for you have found the pathway to
        healing and wholeness.
Blessed are you who have learned from
        your mistakes, and
    have brought them into the light;
    for through regret and forgiveness
        new life is born.
Blessed are you who have developed patience,
    whose actions arise from your
        heart and soul;
    for the art of right timing brings
        fulfillment.
Blessed are you who respect another's being,
    who act not out of anger, jealousy,
        or frustration;
    for you have learned that love is
        ever the answer.
Blessed are you who walk gently upon Earth,
    who recognize your interconnectedness
        with all of life;
    for you are in communion with the
        Heart of creation!

O Silent Friend, where are You when
I am in need,
when my friends have turned from me?
Have You also forgotten me? Where are
You hiding?
Surely You fear not my anger, the
rage that rises up in me!
Is there no one who will stand by me?
Am I doomed forever to darkness?

In my anguish, I heard You call my name;
You spoke to me out of the silence.
Like whispers of the breeze, your words
refreshed me,
they brought me comfort.
With gentle proddings, You helped me see:
I am my own enemy! Through quarrels
and fights
I alienate myself from others, even
from You, my Divine Friend.

When I opened my heart to You, I was
filled with understanding.
O my Friend, help me to live in peace,
to hold my tongue, to resist lashing
out at others.
Be my Strength and my Guide as I make amends,
as I learn to receive the unending love
You have for all!

The Earth is home to all creation,
      to be lovingly cared for by us in
      communion with the Divine Friend.
Praises be to the Creator of the cosmos!
      With grateful hearts, let us
         give thanks!
What other return can we give to
         the One,
      Who continues to gift us with life?
When we open our heart to the Friend,
      when we live with compassion and
         kindness,
      we walk in beauty!
We come to know the Divine Guest,
      Whose companioning Presence
         is ever with us.

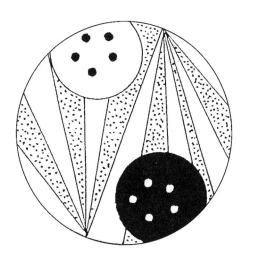

O my Friend, the addictions of this world
           are so misleading;
       they promise delight, yet end in
              corrupting the soul!
In my pride and ignorance, I thought that
       I would not lose myself, that
              I could control my life.
But my cravings only grew, I surrendered
              my will to them;
       I became as empty in spirit as
           an abandoned house.

Having been brought low by my weaknesses,
       I cry out to You for strength and healing,
              though I feel unworthy.
Come to my aid! Help me face all that is
              in darkness within me!
       Help me grow into my full potential!
Let my passion be to share myself and
              my gifts with all,
       ever giving thanks to You,
              my Counselor and my Friend!

*I*s there no time in our lives
        when we are not tested;
    when we are free simply to be
        who we are?
In my early years, I ran with
        the wind,
    I chased butterflies and listened
        to nature's symphony.
            I was free!
Now, all day long I am besieged by
        busyness,
    the business of becoming someone.
            But who?

Bring understanding to my heart, O Friend,
        before I waste away, or become
            like a robot!
        Like an automaton controlled by others!
I yearn to know myself, to discover my
        hidden talents,
    to develop the strengths that will
        bring joy,
    to become a gift shared with others
        that brings blessing.
Awaken me! O loving companion Friend,
            awaken me!

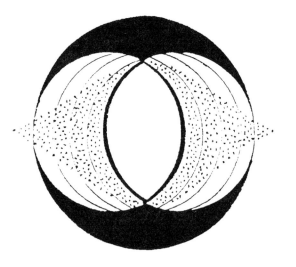

$\mathcal{Y}$our love, O Blessed Companion, reaches into
every open heart,
searching for a welcoming home
like a bird returning to its nest.
For our hearts are the temple of Divine Spirit,
the sacred space of love!

Only the ignorant shut the door to love,
thinking their own power will be
sufficient;
their days are spent walking in darkness;
they feel empty and alone.
Seeking only the world's treasures, which
never satisfy for long,
they are unaware of the true Treasure;
greed and arrogance separate them.

All the while, You, O Blessed One, patiently
await the invitation
to take up residence in their heart,
to open to them as Divine Guest
the wondrous treasures of love.

$\mathcal{I}$direct my concerns to You, O Life
of my life, for
I have learned the power of prayer;
I trust that You know what is best
for me.
When faced with temptation, I quickly
turn to You for help!
Give me strength, O Counselor, to walk away
from that which is wrong,
courage to stand for the right, and
wisdom to know the difference.
Receive my thanks for giving me insight,
for guiding me to the way of life.
Blessed are You, O ever-faithful Friend!

*A*ll praise be to You, O Rudder of
my life,
to You Who instruct my heart
at night, and
keep me on course throughout
the day.
Those who are wise call upon You,
they listen in the silence for
your voice.
They do not await trouble to befriend You;
for You are already known to them,
O loving companion Presence.
Blessed are those who commune with You,
Heart of all hearts!

$\mathcal{I}$ cry out to You, O Friend, when
        illness visits me!
    Make yourself known, for
        I feel so alone.
Even when family and friends try
        to reassure me,
     my fears well up like an army
        to overwhelm me.

Make wise those who attend my needs,
        aspiring to restore me to wholeness.
Pour forth your healing love and light;
       for You are the great Healer,
       the Blessed One Who makes all
         things new.
You bring comfort to the afflicted,
         peace to their souls.

When I cried out, You heard me,
       You answered my call.
With You by my side, O Friend,
       I can weather these dark days,
       I can face whatever the future
         holds.
Blessed are You, Who are loving companion
        to all who call upon You.
      You are the Life of my life!

$\mathcal{Y}$ou are the Light of my life! As the night
            gives way to the sun,
      so You shine into my darkness.
With your light, I confront the shadows
            of fear and ignorance,
      making room for love and creativity.
Then does my spirit soar with abandon;
      I am lifted up as on eagle wings,
            like an angel in flight.

Yes, as my fears and doubts are faced,
      my heart opens like a flower
            in full bloom.
Others are drawn to me, yearning for
            the inward peace of love,
      desiring to cast off the darkness
            of ignorance.
As from a desert waste they come,
      thirsting for the cup of healing,
      hungry for the bread of life.

Blessed are You Who bring light to those
            who walk in darkness,
      love to those who welcome You
            into their heart.
Blessed are You Who illuminate all
                  of creation
      with light and love and power!

$\mathcal{T}$he heavens reflect the magnificence
of creation,
the Earth displays myriad gifts
of the Creator!
Divine love continually emanates out
to the entire universe,
yet how few there are who receive
the gift.

Who will open their hearts to the
blessings of love?
Who will surrender their lives
to be guided by the Spirit?
Who will invite the Most Holy into
the heart's abode,
to take up residence as Friend
and Divine Guide?
Those who befriend the Tender of souls,
will be surprised by the Spirit;
their lives will reflect the kindness
of Divine Love.

*H*ow can I call out to You, O Holy One,
   when I feel so worthless, like a
      castoff faded garment?
When I look in the mirror, I see only
      a stranger,
      a nobody glaring with disgust!
Who is there for the loveless voices
      of the world?

Even amid terrible anguish, I heard
      your gentle voice:
"Do not despair, dear one. I love you
      through all eternity;
      you are gift to me; we belong to
         one another.
Look not at the mirror on the wall. Rather,
      look at your soul's reflection—
         behold your own beauty!
As you nurture the garden within,
      the radiance of soul blossoms will
         shine in loveliness."
Then You did cover me like a blanket
      of blessing and love.
      You filled my heart with hope!

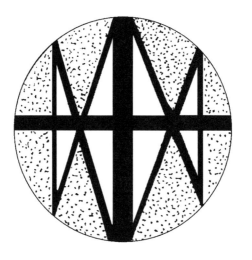

In your Spirit I will take my stand;
    You shine light into the dark
            places of the heart.
Like the sun, You radiate warmth—
        illuminating the shadows of
            fear and ignorance.
Truth finds a home here and
    wise are those who live it!
Let your light penetrate into my
            darkness, O my Friend;
        ignite my soul with the fire
            of your love.
Blessed are all who come to know You
    as the Beloved of their heart!

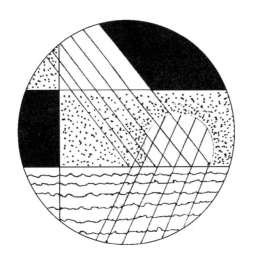

$\mathcal{L}$ike dry ground awaiting the rain,
      so my soul thirsts for the
            Living Waters of love.
What is this poverty of spirit that
         is like a wasteland?
      When did I separate myself from
           your companioning Presence?
I walk by day like one lost in
               a desert,
      void of meaning and purpose;
         the nights are long.
Come! O Fountain of love and grace!
      Come and awaken my spirit!
         Come, refresh my soul!

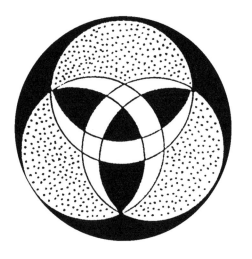

$\mathcal{B}$eloved Friend, You are my hope,
        my comfort and my guide;
     You lead me through troubled times
       on to peaceful paths.
With your strength upholding me, I
       gain courage
   to stand for truth and justice,
   for all that is loving and kind.
Even when I fear death, your love
         suffuses me;
     You help me understand that to die
       to inappropriate habits opens
         the doorway to new life.
You prepare a chapel in my heart,
   a home where I feel secure.
Surely, your loving companion Presence
      will be with me
   all the days of my life and
        forevermore.

O great Architect, You Who set the foundations
            of Earth
        and fashioned infinite galaxies
            in space,
How wondrous that You make our hearts
            your dwelling place;
        You are present, O Divine Guest,
            to all who call upon You!

Awaken us, O Beloved Friend, that we in turn
            befriend all of creation—
        rooting out our inner fears,
        lovingly respecting Earth's creatures
            and resources.
Blessed are those who open wide
            the heart's door!
        They will come to understand
            the language of love,
        they will be united with You!

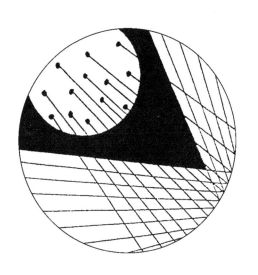

O Merciful One, pour forth your healing
    light and abiding promise
        into my heart;
For You are my hope and my life!
    In You and through You I will
        become whole.
Even when I stumble and turn from You,
        when I lose the way—
    You watch over me with infinite
        patience.
You are eager to welcome me home with
        abiding love;
    You rejoice in my return!
O Blessed One, as I open my heart
        to your grace,
    may others also receive blessings
        of the Holy Mystery.

$\mathcal{B}$eloved Friend, how I want to spend time
    with those who speak truth and
        who live with integrity.
Help me choose the path of wholeness
    placing my trust in You.

The ways of those who do not call upon
      your guiding love are often
        tempting;
They seem to promise fun and
        happiness,
    lives of excitement and ease.
Yet, I have seen how that path leads
        to trouble;
    loneliness and insecurity soon
        follow.

So I turn to You for strength in
        testing times;
    guide my steps toward wisdom.
If I stumble and lose the way,
        hasten!
    Pluck me up from temptation's snare.
      Set me on the path of love!
For You are my Guide and my Friend.

$\mathcal{Y}$ou, O Unseen Companion, are the
        Strength of my life;
    wherever I go, You are with me.
Like a good father You guide and protect me;
    with a mother's love You bring
            comfort and healing.
    Of whom shall I be afraid?

When my parents and friends do not
            understand me,
    when I feel lonely and doubt my
            own worth,
You are like a rock, a foundation
            built on love within me;
    my fears melt away.
Then courage and confidence rise up
            in triumph;
    once again, my heart rests in a
            peace beyond understanding.

*H*eart of all hearts, I cry out to You;
    do not remain silent in me,
        for confusion rules my life!
When unkind and hurtful words pour
        from my mouth,
    I cannot seem to stop them.
Relief comes, yet my heart is heavy
        with shame;
    I feel so alone in my misery.
Friends and family alike seem to
        shun me.
    I don't even like myself!

Hear my plea, be close to me as
    I wrestle with my unbridled
        tongue!
For I know You are the source of
        wisdom and truth;
    counsel me that the fogs of fear
        and pain might lift.
Help me to face the source of this anger
        and to make amends.
With your love I know forgiveness,
    my heart will once again feel light.

$\mathcal{T}$he Divine Guest lives within your heart;
blessed are you who listen for
love's secret voice.
Even a whisper from the voice of love
is powerful,
uprooting fear and melting
hearts of stone.
Gratitude and songs of joy fill you
as you befriend the Beloved
of your heart.

*B*lessed are You, Who understand my tears,
    You comfort me with love's embrace.
Though my eyes cannot see You,
    I feel your gentle Presence,
    like angel wings lifting my spirit.
Your love is awesome, too great
        to comprehend.

When I rebel and do that which I know
        in my heart is wrong,
    a cloud hangs about me;
        I walk as in a fog,
        I weep with regret.
Then I turn again to You for solace,
    and know the freedom that comes
        from forgiveness.
You turn my mourning into joy,
    I dance to a new song.
Blessed are You, O loving Companion
        of my heart.

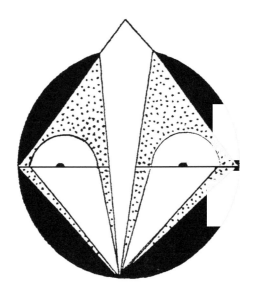

$\mathscr{B}$lessed One, come to me! For my mind
is muddled,
filled with fear and conflict!
How does one find the road that leads
to wholeness,
or stand firm when drawn to
crooked paths?

So often I feel like a tiny speck,
unseen and unheard;
Then I succumb to temptation;
I become loud and rebellious that
others will take note of me;
Neither way reverences You or myself,
O Friend.

Yet, when I am still, when I listen
quietly,
your voice within instructs me!
"Recognize your worthiness, you
who demean yourself!
Bless the special gifts you bring to
share with the world!
Honor who you are: a unique spark
of Divine Love!
Awaken to your birthright:
peace, assurance, love, joy—
and give thanks!"

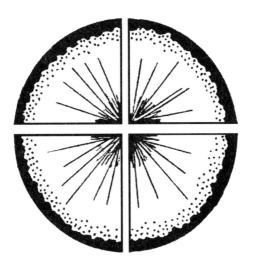

$\mathcal{B}$lessed are you whose wrongdoings
    have been forgiven,
  whose guilt has melted into joy.
Blessed are you who live with confidence,
  who courageously stand for truth—
    strong and tall as a mighty tree
      with respect for all life.

You who hide with shame separate yourself
    from the true Friend,
  fear and loneliness companion you;
  bitterness blocks love's forgiving
    word.
Even then the Heart of all hearts waits.
  As you turn to love with regret,
    your heart is make clean.
You are freed from the heavy weight
    of guilt and illusion
  to soar like an eagle in the wind,
  to live harmoniously with life
    itself!
Blessed are you who gently walk the
    path of truth!

O, how good to give thanks and praise
to You, O Creator,
You Who made the entire universe
by the power of love!
When You speak, it comes to pass:
heavens studded with suns, moons,
stars, and planets;
Earth abounding in minerals, plants,
and animals—
life beyond measure!

How is it that humankind seems no longer
to reverence this wondrous gift
of love?
O, Life of all lives, awaken your people!
Open our heart's eyes and ears
that we turn the tide of desecration
to the healing of our Earth home!
Then will our hearts be glad and songs
of joy rise up;
We will give thanks to You, Who are
ever-ready
to guide and direct us in the
great dance of life!

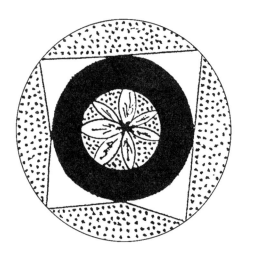

$\mathcal{H}$appy am I that You are my Friend,
    You Who dwell in my heart,
    You Who celebrate my growth and
        stand by me in stressful times.
When I was but a child, I cried out
            to You
    when fears awakened me at night,
    when I felt powerless by day.
Your loving Presence comforted me,
        and I felt secure.

Through your love, I learn kindness,
        patience, and tolerance;
    even parents, teachers, and friends
        notice the changes in me.
Truly, as I come to understand myself,
    as I allow You to direct and
        guide my life,
Challenges are met, problems melt away;
    I no longer fear the future;
        now is sufficient for the day!
Yes, happy are all who know You as Friend.

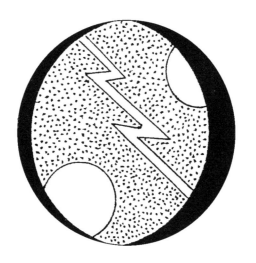

$\mathcal{P}$ray with me, O Strong Friend, for I am
         filled with fury!
     Arrows of spite and malice have
             pierced my heart!
Shaking and trembling, I want only to
             answer in kind—to retaliate;
     yet knowing, in truth, that will not
             bring peace.
Anger begets anger, and like a boomerang
         soon returns to its home.

I cry out to You! Pour your strength
             into my heart;
     give me courage to stand for love
             and truth.
Through your love forgive those who
                 wrong me,
         those who abuse me;
     let peace come to those who hate.
May those who find pleasure in hurting
             others be humbled
     and turn their hearts to You.
May your light increase and overcome
                 ignorance!
     May love break through hearts of fear!
Great are You, O Peacemaker, my Strength,
         and my Friend.

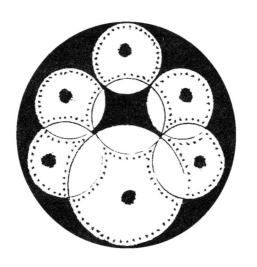

*H*ow precious is your loving Presence,
          O companioning Friend!
      A refuge in troubling times.
Through your love comes every good thing;
        we feast on Earth's abundance,
        living streams of water quench
            our thirst;
For You are the very Source of life.

Yet how often we turn our backs to You;
        ignorance and fear take residence
           in our hearts,
        we feel lonely even amid friends.
O Friend of my heart, protect me from
           the pressure of peers,
        from those who live in the wilderness
           of addictions.
Awaken those who live in darkness, that
        they might bask in your love,
           and live in your light.

$\mathcal{T}$rust in the Holy One and live with love,
  ever in harmony with nature,
      enjoying Earth's bounty —
        the vast variety of her riches.
Be not like those who exploit others,
    who live by greed and deceit,
      who take without return;
For the spirit of the selfish is weak,
        and eventually broken.

The upright of heart follow the path of love,
    with kindness and understanding they
        are blessing to the world;
In times of trouble, love is their
          stronghold,
      the Beloved Friend leading them
        safely home.

Puffed up with pride, the greedy are like
        inflated balloons,
      hot air that soon bursts or
          fizzles out.
Those who plant seeds of love in their hearts
    soon reap a harvest of delight;
      blessings are the blossoms they enjoy
        and bring as gift to the world.

To whom can I turn when I feel so alone?
　　When life seems so unfair and
　　　friends, teachers, and family know
　　　　　not my deepest fears?
Looking into the mirror, I see a stranger!
　　　As my body changes, I feel awkward,
　　　　　like a puzzle with missing pieces.
I ask myself over and over, who am I?
　　　Will I ever burst from this cocoon?
　　　　Who will I become?

In desperation I cry out to You, my Friend.
　　　I wait for your loving Presence
　　　　to enfold me.
All my fears are known to You; even if
　　　I were to run,
　　　I cannot hide from your love —
　　　　for You live in me.

You speak to me within my heart:
　　　"Trust in who you are becoming,
　　　　　my friend;
　　　Always live and walk your own truth.
Know yourself as a beloved child of
　　　the universe,
　　　loved beyond measure just as you are.
　　　　And be at peace."

O Beloved Friend, why did no one warn me
of life's sufferings,
of the agonies of growing up?
Joy and freedom were the ways of
childhood,
carefree days of running with the wind,
of companionship with creation.
When did fear begin to rule my life—
so many, I cannot name them all?
Surely one can slow this mad pace,
this rush to maturity;
surely stress is not a friend!

You have given us free will, the capacity
to create our life;
yet so many, like me, get caught
in the world's torrent,
like ships headed for disaster.

O my Friend, give me the strength and
discipline to stop, to
listen for your voice in the silence.
Be my Guide and Counselor, that I may
choose a gentler path,
that I might realign myself in harmony
with nature's seasons.
Surely then I will be blessed in all I do,
and blessing to those I meet on
life's highway.
Thanks be to You, who I call Friend!

Come, O my Friend, hear my prayer;
      for fear would make a home
            in me.
Come, make haste to help me.
      Let my fears be put to rest.

Come, O my Friend, stay close by;
      for with You hidden in my heart,
            I have the key to life!
My fears fly away; your love
            remains with me.

Come, O my Friend. Live in my heart
            forever and ever.

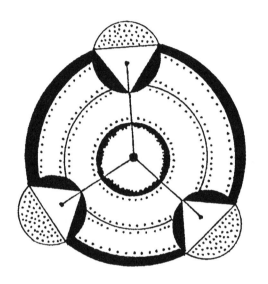

$\mathcal{B}$lessed are you who help others,
    those who are in need.
For as you offer your presence,
        you come to know the
        Divine Guest in your heart.

Even when your friends are unkind
        to you,
    when they ignore or tease
        you,
Do not become mean or spiteful.
    Rather, send them love and
        imagine light around them.
Kindness comes from love, and
    those who practice love
        will be blessed.

Sometimes I cry at night for all
        I do not understand—
                I feel so alone.
Then, as if in parents' arms,
        or held in angel wings,
                waves of love enfold me.

I think, "This must be the Friend,
        the One I knew even before
                my birth."
Then my tears turn to smiles; for
        I know I am not alone.

"Thank you," I whisper into the
                silence of the night,
        and sleep with peaceful
                heart
Until the dawning of a new day.

$\mathcal{W}$hy does life seem so unfair
        at times?
    You, who are my unseen Friend,
        help me understand.
When I talk with You in my heart,
    I feel safety in your love.
Yet, when fears arise, I wonder,
        "Do You hear me?"

Cover me with your kindness,
        wrap around me a blanket
            of love.
When I can't have my own way,
        show me what is best
            for me.
Help me see that with You in
        my heart,
    no one, not anything, can
        separate our friendship.

Even when You seem far away,
        You are here:
    a mystery to my understanding.
O, my Friend, stay close by and
        I shall not be afraid.
I will become all that You created
        me to be
    as You guide me on the way.

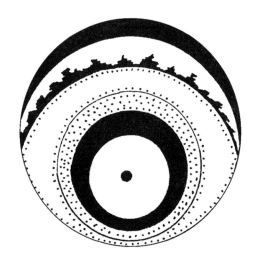

Remember, O precious one, to listen
      with your heart's ear, to see
            with your heart's eye.
While the eyes and ears of the body
      hear and see the beauty
            of the Earth,
Those of the heart hear and come
            to recognize the
      voice of the Friend who is
            ever-present to you.

The inward voice of the Beloved points
            to simple things:
      wind whispering through trees,
      snow patterns on window panes . . .
            secrets of the heart.
The Earth is the playground of
            the great Friend.
      Care for it, O child of Earth,
            that it might always
                  lovingly care for you.

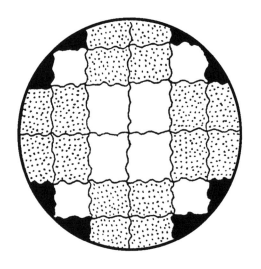

$\mathcal{H}$appy are those who know love in
their hearts!
They bring peace and joy
to others;
They face life's obstacles and
struggles
with patience and trust.
Opening their hearts to the Friend,
they learn to look for blessings—
even in times of trouble.

With gladness and joy they
listen quietly for the gentle
voice of the Friend
within.
As migrating birds fly directly to
their winter homes,
so those who dwell with love
are led to safe places.
Instead of a house of fear, they
live secure,
giving thanks to the One who
abides in their hearts
forever.

$\mathcal{I}$n You I feel safe, O my Friend,
     You are a loving Presence
         in times of need.
Therefore, I shall not fear when
         troubles arise.

There is a secret room in my heart,
     the hidden home of the Friend:
You are ever with us; You gently
         nudge us
     toward our own unique gifts; thus,
     we live into our special calling.
Yes, You companion us forever—
     our assurance, our strength,
         and our joy.
Thanks be to You, Heart of all hearts!

Clap your hands, all peoples!
Praise the Holy One with
songs of joy!
For the Divine Guest, Holy Wisdom,
is powerful,
the great unifier of all the
Earth.

Love is like the glue of the universe
binding all things together.
When love breaks through our fears,
old wounds are eased,
peace fills our hearts.
Clap your hands, all peoples!
Praise the Holy One with
songs of joy!
Dance to the rhythm of the universe!

$\mathcal{B}$lessed are You, Friend of our hearts,
  and greatly to be praised!
For You are the Most High;
   You created the heavens and
    all the Earth;
Yet You make your home in our
    hearts.

Sometimes I wonder how it is
    that You,
   Who are so mighty, come
   to live in our small hearts.
Why do our hearts not break?
Yet is this not the Mystery of love,
  the gift given to all?
Blessed are You! and greatly to
    be praised!

*W*hy should I give up in times
                of darkness,
        when a crowd of fears
                threaten me—
Fears that separate me from all
        I aspire to become?
Turning to You, O Friend, to
                guide me
        is my strength and support,
        a stronghold in difficult times.

Be not afraid to seek the Treasure
                within,
        to discover the beauty hidden
                in the heart's garden.
For as you root out the weeds of fear,
        peace, love, truth, and joy
                begin to flower;
Light radiates out from your
        inner garden to all the world.

$\mathcal{T}$he Creator, through the energy
of love,
brought forth the world.
From the rising of the sun to a new dawn,
love radiates out to all people,
to the earth, perfect
in beauty.
Be glad! The Friend is ever beaming
love into each heart;
those who welcome the Friend,
who listen for the heart's voice
in silence, and
who heed love's call,
Will know peace, gratitude, and
assurance;
they will walk in love's light.

$\mathcal{H}$ow can I turn to You, O blessed Healer,
      when I feel so ashamed,
    when I am forced to face my scheming
      petty smallness of heart?
Answer me, You Who are gracious and kind
      to the humble of heart,
    to all who cry out for mercy and healing.
Because of my ignorance and self-centeredness,
      I live in fear;
    like a coward, I bully others so that
      I might feel strong.

Hear my plea, O Compassionate Friend,
      as I bow my head in prayer and
          repentance.
Create in me a loving heart, a kind nature;
      stay close by as I face the
        shadows within,
    the fears that weaken me.
Blessed are You, most merciful Friend;
      You heed the wounded and
        contrite of heart.

$\mathcal{L}$ike a child playing in water and
 building castles in the sand,
I want to live peacefully with a
 joyful heart,
 free from turmoil and fear.
So I call upon You, O Divine Guest!
 Build a strong house within me.
Fill it with strength and courage,
 trim it with beauty,
 surround it with love and light.
Send your angels to protect it,
 to guide my life that I may be
 a peaceful presence
 in the world.

$\mathcal{B}$lessed are those who come to prayer
     with openness of heart,
       silently listening for the still,
         small voice within.
Freely abandoning themselves to You,
       O Heart of Love,
      they rest secure and find refreshment
       for their soul.
In this love-centered prayer, they come
        to know You, to look for You
    within others and all of creation—
        yes, even within their enemies.
Grant, O Friend, that I learn to pray
         simply,
    to surrender my heart, my mind,
       my will, into your hands;
For, I, too, yearn to be a loving presence
     in the world.

O Spirit of Truth, enter my mind.
Awaken me from ignorance,
enfold me in silence;
May all that I speak bring healing
and light.
Be Thou my mind, O Divine Light!

O Soul of Wisdom, enter my heart.
Cleanse me of illusion, and
free me from fear;
May I become a life-giving presence,
a blessing to others.
Be Thou my heart, O Holy Guest!

$\mathcal{H}$ow can I commune with You, O Beloved,
  when fear keeps welling up to
       confuse and distract me?
When I look around, I see the rooms
       of my house
    reflect the disorder of my mind!
Who could find peace in such chaos?

O my Friend, counsel and guide me as
    I create a sacred space
       within my heart,
    a place where divine love reigns.
Quell the noisy fears; teach me
    to see with the eye of the heart,
    to hear with the heart's ear.
May beauty replace the squalor of
       unbridled thoughts,
    may peace become a constant
       companion.

*B*eloved of my heart, be my witness as
      I face the fears that separate me
          from your love;
For I yearn to be a beneficial presence
        in the world,
        not one whose light is dim.

Teach me to love the creatures
        of your world;
        keep me from harming any of them.
Help me understand the interconnectedness
        of all things, that
        I live with compassion and delight
          in the diversity of life.

May your light shine through me
        awakening others;
        may your love in me radiate blessing.
All praise be to You, Heart of creation!

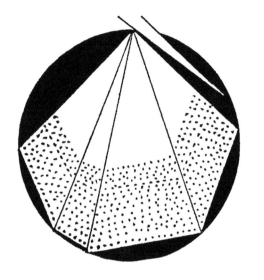

$\mathscr{B}$reathe deeply, for the breath is life!
Take time to bask in the silence
of your heart,
for Earth and heaven meet here.
The heart and mind are one in the
still point of love,
the abode where your ills are healed,
where you are bathed in forgiveness.
Befriend the Beloved of your heart,
Who is the Breath of your breath,
the Life of your life—
and give thanks!

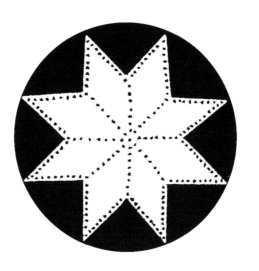

O that I might learn to listen to
Your still, quiet voice within
my heart.
For You come to all who welcome You,
to those who await your counsel
and guidance.
All I will ever need, therefore,
is within me!
Teach me to stand firm like the
mountain,
to flow like a gentle stream,
to bend like a willow in all
of life's storms.
May I become as strong and courageous
as lion,
gentle as doe, free and farseeing
as eagle.
Thus, I will walk through my fears—a
witness to love's transforming power!

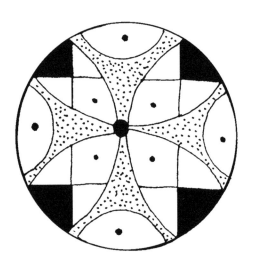

$\mathcal{W}$hy do I feel forlorn and disquieted,
O Blessed One?
Has the joy I have known flown
away forever?
Awaken me, O You Who never sleep!
Help me see with clarity
the root of this distress.

In the silence my heart trembled
and quaked;
as past thoughts and deeds welled up,
I wept with deep remorse.
Then I cried out to You for forgiveness,
desiring to make amends, to walk
once again on peaceful paths.

All praise be to You, O Mender of
our brokenness—
to You Who gather the fragments
of our lives and
fashion them anew in beauty!

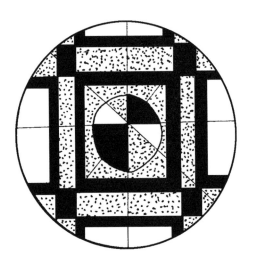

Gracious and merciful are You,
  O Healer of broken hearts, and
    greatly to be praised!
When my stubborn desires refuse
    to give way to truth,
  when I finally fall like
    humpty dumpty from the wall,
You pick up the pieces of my life;
  You fashion them together
    with love.
O Blessed Friend, continue to humble me
  as I learn the ways of Holy Wisdom;
  may I become a beam of love
    on the freedom road to life.

O Blessed One, where are You hiding
    as our world seems bent on violence
        and destruction?
Gone are times of silence and simplicity,
    where soul-dreams were heard
        in the night,
        where life missions were made clear—
            guided by the heart's voice.

Come, O Great Dreamer! Awaken us from
        our numb sleep!
    Let the nightmares of greed, fear,
        and aggression
    be brought into your light.
Make known your divine dream to all
        humanity;
        arouse all of creation to love's way!
Then will planet Earth sing new melodies—
    songs of peace, joy, and blessing.

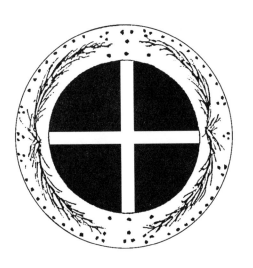

O Beloved of all hearts, how I yearn
to bask in your love!
To walk by faith rather than fear—
to be a companioning friend
to You.
For far too long I have felt unworthy,
like an orphan unwanted and alone,
Forgetting that You call me by name;
You shelter me in the palm of
your hands!
Like all who open the heart's door,
You are mine; I am Yours!
O Beloved Friend, quiet my restless soul;
may I ever remember that my
true home is love.
Thanks be to You, Who are love!

O my Friend, You stand like a lighthouse
as we voyage through life,
as we embark on the sea of
the unknown.
The beacon of your light charts our way,
that we may travel safely,
with clear direction.
Your faithful love strengthens and
comforts us
when the journey seems long
and too lonely;
And your power is awesome, assuring us
when dark waters roil and threaten.
O Beloved, with You as our helmsman
we shall reach the furthest shore;
You will welcome us home with
laughter and joy!

O Compassionate Creator, You who brought
        forth the universe
    with love, and light, and power,
    we are sorely in need of rebirth.
Have mercy on your people, forgive us
        our wanton ways;
    let us not make of Earth a wasteland.
May the beauty and majesty of your handiwork
        stand forever, that
    every generation to come will live
        with wonder, that they
    may enjoy the fruits of this,
        your gift of life.

$\mathcal{I}$ turn to You, O Wisdom of all ages,
        for counsel and guidance;
    my life is in turmoil, every moment
        filled with busyness.
We who live in time and space seem
        headed for breakdown,
    like rockets spinning out of control.

All our good works have little meaning
      without your love and light
        to empower them.
May we slow down and learn once again
      the wisdom of silence,
      the efficacy of simplicity,
      the renewal of solitude,
That we might be co-partners with You
      in healing and re-creating
        planet Earth,
      blue-green jewel afloat in
        the universal sea.

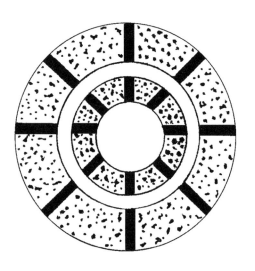

Come, O Comforter! for I am filled
with fears
as I face the unknown,
as I place myself in the hands
of the surgeon.
Come, O angels! Enfold me in your wings.
Bring peace to my heart, and
guide all who attend
the afflicted.
Come, O Healer! Renew my spirit,
that all within me may be
made whole; that
I might once again serve You
with strength and zeal.
All praise and gratitude be to You,
O Blessed One, to You
Who lead us through life's trials,
and live within us forever as
loving companion Presence.

O Beloved Friend, at times your love
seems too much for me;
I feel unworthy and turn from You.
Then I become like a hot air balloon,
raising myself above others;
I boast and seek attention
wherever I go.
Yet doubt and loneliness are constant
companions;
inwardly, I am deflated, empty and
secretly ashamed,
forgetting that I am already loved
by You, without condition.
Come, O true Friend! Raise me up from
this pit of my own making!

Blessed are all who awaken to your love,
your enduring companion Presence,
within their hearts!

O Divine Lover, fill the hearts of your people
with compassion and mercy;
burn away our fears and doubts
with your fire!
O Wisdom of the ages, open our heart's eyes,
beam light into the darkness of ignorance.
Awaken us that oppression and injustice
might cease!

How long! How long will our wanton ways,
our apathy, mediocracy, and squandering
of resources go on?
Daughters of love, sons of light, arise!
Teach us songs that enlighten the soul;
reconnect our spirits to the holy
oneness of all creation!
For darkness reigns over the world in
these times.
Yet the light shall free us from
darkness as
we choose the way of truth.
May it soon be so!

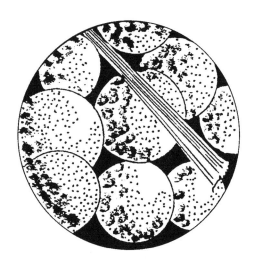

O Eternal Counselor, You are the source
of all understanding;
awaken your people, the leaders of
nations, to Earth's cry!
For, despite institutions of learning,
the darkness of ignorance grows;
fear and violence are rampant.
Of what use are schools and certificates
if common courtesy and kindness
have been forgotten,
if the interconnectedness of all life
is not central?
What is to be gained through study and testing
when minds are numbed by excess, or
deluded through illusive desires,
when peace is preached, yet weapons
of war prevail?
O Compassionate Healer, have mercy!
Come with hosts of angels
to open all hearts to the Great Mystery,
the oneness of being,
O that the energies of integrity and
wholeness would
radiate around the globe!

$\mathcal{W}$e cry out to You, O Cosmic Creator!
  Awaken us to our sacred belonging
      to all life, for
  NOW is the time to fulfill our
        birthright.
Fear and doubt bar the gateway to
      wholeness, to
  expressing peace and compassion.
Break through our resistance;
    be our strength as we reconcile
      the darkness with the light.
For as we live in harmony, we radiate
      peace to the world;
    as we know who and Whose we are,
      compassion becomes our way.
All praise be to You, O Gracious Mirror
      of our lives.

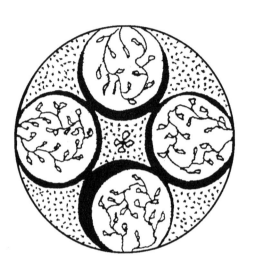

O Beloved Friend, Source of all creation,
blessed are we as
You companion us from earthly birth
to rebirth into the heavenly abode.
Is it not life's journey to grow in love:
to learn to care for one another
even as You care for us . . .
to attend to all creation with reverence,
wisdom, and integrity?
Is it not our aspiration to awaken fully
to the sacredness of everything,
to the oneness of all united in love?
O, friends of the Friend, let us awaken
to our birthright!
Let us claim peace and harmony among
ourselves and the nations!
Let us stand united in our diversity
as we spread blessings to all.

$\mathcal{H}$ave mercy, O Compassionate Companion!
　　We, who would serve creation,
　　　　are surrounded by chaos;
　　the darkness of greed and violence
　　　　　　seem to reign.
Fear radiates out like tentacles of octopi
　　squeezing the hearts of your people.
Come! Have mercy! Renew our souls!
　　Awaken our spirits to love!

For, truly, love is the one law of life.
　　When our minds and our hearts express
　　　　　love's law,
　　our lives reflect new vistas of
　　　　wonder, peace, and freedom.
We delight in lives of service, co-creating
　　　　in communion with you, divine source
　　　　of all being, Holy Wisdom,
　　　　　　Beloved Guest of our heart.

O friends, let us open our minds and
our hearts
to explore the Mystery: our inner
beings, our outer challenges;
let us face the obstacles and veils
to freedom and wonder.
Be not afraid of change! For still ponds
become stagnant
when not quickened and nourished
by hidden streams.
O Blessed One, enliven us with living
streams of your mercy.
Cast off our outworn garments of fear
and judgment, and
adorn us with the light of awakened
consciousness!
O Divine Guest, dream your Dream in us!
Instruct us in the wisdom of the heart,
our interconnecting center with
Divine Love,
that we may join with You in the
great song of creation!

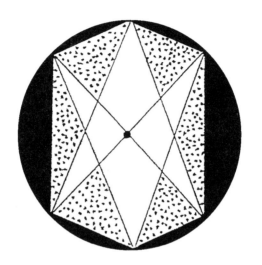

O Eternal Friend, my life is in shambles;
   chaos reigns without, disharmony within!
   Where is the flow of peace and balance
            I once knew?
How can I know your blessed Presence when
      I rush about trying to keep pace
            with the world,
Setting aside the aspirations of my heart
      for the lure of busyness and desire?

O Holy Counselor, help me to choose wisdom,
      to stop the infernal race to "success"
            and to rest peacefully in
               the eternal now.
Only then will harmony be regained and
               balance restored;
      only then will integrity return and
      joy radiate out to bless others.
Come, O Holy Wisdom! Illuminate my heart
            that I may see!

O friends, be not anxious about the past,
for whatever was is gone;
worry not about the future, tomorrow
has yet to be created.
Be ever mindful of the eternal now, for
all you think and feel and do
creates your future;
the present moment is yours to choose.

Abandon yourself to the divine laws of love;
thus will peace, order, and assurance
bless your life.
Surrender to the Divine Light within,
where wisdom dwells; listen for the
still, small voice, the inner Counselor,
Whose truth will set you free
that your soul might soar.

$\mathcal{B}$eloved are You, Blessed Friend, to those
    who awaken to love and light,
    who come to hear your voice
        in the silence.
You send angels to guide us on the journey,
    to assist us over obstacles that
        block our path.
Happy are those who learn to ask,
    who heed messages that come in
        countless ways, and
    who give thanks to the angelic
        realm among us.
For those who know heaven's company
    become partners in communion
        with the Divine Plan for
            Earth and humanity.

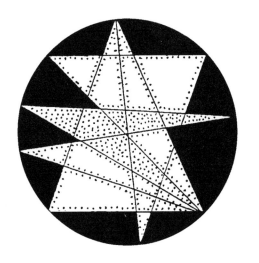

O friends of the Beloved, awaken to the
power of thought!
Do you not know that what you think is
like a prayer?
That your every thought is heard,
and, in time, becomes reality
rebounding back to you?
Therefore, be mindful! Let your thinking
come from the heart, from
the source of divine intelligence.
Learn to speak out of the deep silence,
where the Word springs forth,
where fear-thoughts are transmuted
into blessing as you offer
them up to the light.

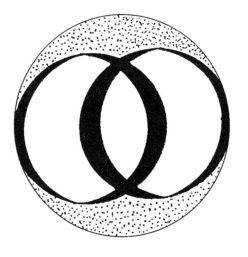

$\mathcal{T}$hose who live with inner peace, in harmony
with others and the earth,
Will come to know divine harmony and will
delight in the interconnectedness and
beauty of creation.
No longer will they fear the differences
of race, creed, or color;
they will enjoy the rich tapestry
of diversity, and celebrate
the sacred beauty of each unique being.

Blessed are those who unite in
the great work.
For they will help create a world of light
and love that will vibrate
in harmony with the music of the cosmos.
They will radiate peace to the world and
will live at one with You,
O Holy Wisdom,
Heart of all hearts!

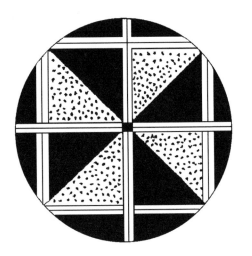

Awakening to each new day, O friends,
we are born anew; as
we choose daily to release our
inner places of darkness,
to die to old habits and attitudes,
light enters there.
Listen to the Word enscrolled upon your heart,
the daily bread that makes all
things new and, like sunshine,
radiates out to a soul-sick world.
Let all who yearn to become chalices of peace
abandon themselves to light, love, and life,
becoming bearers of beauty, truth,
blessing, and goodness.
Blessed are You, O companioning Presence!
You answer those who call to You,
those who aspire to grow into living
blossoms of beauty.

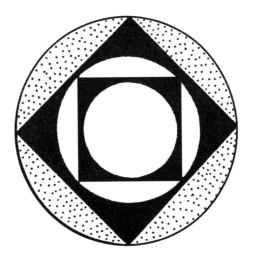

$\mathcal{W}$ondrous are You, O Great Conductor of
the universal symphony!
For You create beauty and harmony
even in the midst of our ignorance
and chaos.
To each individual a key is given to unlock
its own unique sound.
What notes will your song add to
the cosmic composition?
How will the sound of your voice
and being bless the Earth?
Listen! Listen well! For creation's song
we all yearn to sing, the
hymn of the universe, echoes deeply
in the silence of our own souls.

O Great Mender of souls, we long to be
loved, to be understood.
Create in us the humility, strength,
and courage
to seek reconciliation, to heal the
wounds of separation.
Blessed are those who know the grace
of forgiveness, for
their capacity to give and receive
love is expanded;
their souls are unbound, healed,
and released to soar.
Through forgiveness comes liberation,
the freedom to receive God's grace,
the desire to share and extend love.
Seek then the One Who knows all hearts;
ask forgiveness of all that
separates you from love.
Rejoice! For what was broken will be
made whole!
Give thanks to the Beloved, Who is
merciful and kind!

$\mathcal{B}$eloved of my heart, I yearn to anchor
        myself in your love,
    to become ever-more vigilant to
        my soul's growth,
    dying a little each day to all
        that separates and divides.
Prod me, O Divine Guest, to take time each
        day to pray a while,
    to establish a rhythm of silence,
        work, recreation, and being,
    to connect to You, the deepest source
        of my life.
Only then will I live less in time and
    more in the present moment;
    here all things are one and
        I become the prayer.

O my Friend, thank You for angels
that pray over me
when I am too weary from struggle,
conflict, and pain.
O Blessed One, thank You for the wisdom
that illuminates my soul,
transforming my weaknesses into
strength;
Your Light penetrates my fears,
Your Love gentles my anxieties.
As I abandon myself into your heart,
I soar as on eagle wings;
I am free!
I rest peacefully embraced in the
arms of love.
All praises be to You, Light of
all light, Love of all loves!

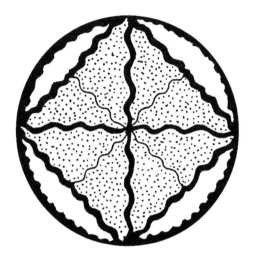

$\mathcal{I}$ come to You, O Life of my life,
        just as I am—
    like a tree in the winter, stark
                and uncovered,
    vulnerable and quiet as new
        growth gestates.
In due season, You will awaken in me
    all that has been dormant,
            asleep in my soul.
The sap of my spirit will rise up,
    quickening the tender shoots that
            will bear sweet fruit.
O gentle Gardener, blessed are You,
        Who prune and tend each tree with
            utter care and boundless love!

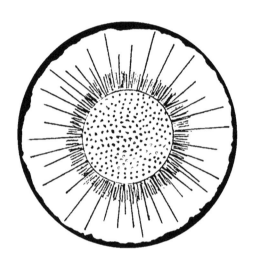

Infinite and eternal Friend, I surrender
all that I am into your heart.
Brand me with the fire of your love!
Sear away the dross: the veils of doubt,
ignorance, and illusion.
For You alone do I desire! You alone
can satisfy this terrible yearning!
As I die daily to all that separates, as
I become an empty vessel—
Fill me! Fill me!
Melt me! Mold me! until I no longer am I,
but I am in communion with You,
Beloved and Lover,
one heart.

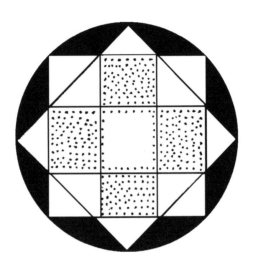

*P*raise the Creator, Light of the universe!
Extol the One Mind, the All of
all that is!
O, that we might awaken to this oneness,
and know ourselves in communion
with You.
Let us be mindful that our thoughts are
our prayer;
they create our very life and being.

Be still then. In the silence become empty;
let us create space for Holy Wisdom
to enter in and through us,
expanding our horizons.
Here we will be peaceful, calm, in harmony
with the universe;
in unity with all beings,
Heaven and Earth will be united in us.
We will be one with love and light.

$\mathcal{W}$hen I was lonely, separated from You,
O Friend,
I wept in despair and sorrow,
weary of suffering.
I cried out to You for solace.
Finally, my tears spent, your gentle voice
whispered within the chalice of
my heart,
You comforted me as a child embraced
by a mother's love.

For that moment, I died to self-centeredness,
allowing your grace to mold me,
to redirect my thoughts to peaceful
and steady paths.
You humbled me so my heart could expand;
You cast out jealousy and envy,
those impediments to peace
of heart and mind.
I basked in the suffusion of your love!
Thus, I discovered the joy of your
loving companion Presence, and
how needful I am of your guiding hand.

$\mathcal{B}$lessed are You, Who invite us
        to wholeness,
    Who see through our masks and
        rationalizations, yet
    Who love us beyond what we could
        ask or imagine!
All praises be to You, Who sustain us,
    Who send angels to guide, protect,
            and awaken us,
    Who forgive our selfish ways and
        renew our lives!
Blessed are we, when we receive your
        bountiful gifts,
    when we call upon You and
        cooperate with your messengers,
    when we are free from fear and live
        as your friends, O Beloved
        of our hearts and souls!

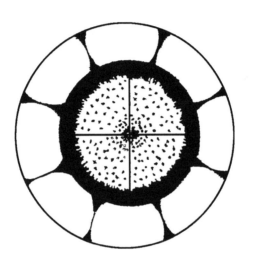

O friends, listen to the promptings of
your heart.
For truth makes itself known in
sacred silent spaces.
Your soul is nurtured in quietude and
with prayer,
ever awaiting seed sown by the Spirit
in fertile heart-soil.
When the distractions of the noisy world
separate us from the Source,
our souls wither;
we forget our purpose: to express
our unique gifts of love,
to blossom in beauty.
O, let us pause in our busy lives; and
let us take gentle moments of being
in the silence,
to listen for the Beloved's voice,
to know love's companioning Presence.

O Creator of infinite variety,
Your Presence graces every work—
      even where we least expect it,
            even as we seem to fail.
For is not each person fashioned
            uniquely in your Plan,
      a special work of art whose
            birthright is love?
Help us, O Great Artist, to weave
            our work and our lives
      into a tapestry that radiates
            beauty, light, and love.

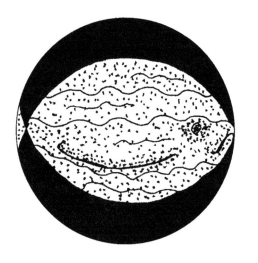

O You, Who pray in all open hearts,
    help me to know and to heed
        your Will;
Flow through me like a river,
    a cleansing and purifying stream.
I rejoice as You commune with my soul
    by day and all through the night.
You shed light on my weaknesses;
    You encourage my strengths.
May my deepest prayer ever be
    to become one with your Will;
    as I remain silent before You,
        I offer You my heart.
Pray through me, Breath of my breath.
    Your prayer is love!

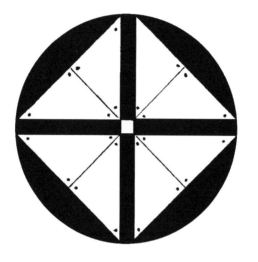

O my Rock, my Counselor, how is it
        I feel so alone—
    even with family and friends who
          love me?
What is the purpose of life in a world
      so filled with violence and greed?
Even when I pray to You and offer You
        my thanksgiving, so often
All seems dry and empty, barren as a desert.
     Where are You in all of this?

"O, dear one, do you not know,
        has no one told you—
You are here to learn of love and light!
I will fill your empty spaces with love,
     I will bring light into the dark places,
        as you learn to heed my Word.
Then, little by little, day by day,
     you will come to live in joy, the freedom
       of all who choose a life
         in communion with me,
     aspiring to make this world heaven
       on Earth.
Listen and know! I am with you always!"

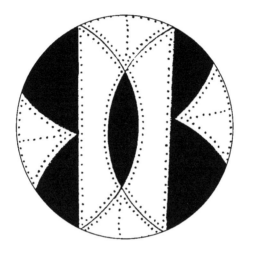

O how I long to spend time just basking
in nature's plentitude,
delighting in the splendor of creation!
There, amid wild flowers and birdsong,
I sense your Presence, O Friend to all.
I am at peace, I am at home.

Yet, the busyness of life distracts me,
I am pulled in every direction—
moving toward what end?
Even in the night, I am restless,
my mind leaping toward tomorrow.
Help me to slow down, O Blessed One,
to choose only life-giving activities
that reflect your Will for me,
that balance and renew my life.
For then, I will be in harmony with You,
with myself, and with creation.
I will join in the song and dance
of Life!

O my friends, close your ears to the
                mind-pollution of gossip,
        to the harmful violence in the media!
For all such reckless talk and intake
                        soils the soul and,
        like an echo, reverberates—
        spreading poison, not love.
Let what you take into your heart and mind
        be for nourishment, joy, and
                understanding,
        that wisdom and wholeness might increase.
Become like a rose in full bloom sending forth
                beauty and serenity to a world
        where darkness seems to flourish;
for peace, assurance, and blessing companion
        those who speak with kindness and care.
        They recognize Holy Wisdom at work
                in the world and in others;
        they are true friends of the Beloved.

$\mathcal{B}$lessed are you who listen to the indwelling
Divine Guest whispering
the Word that is etched upon every
open heart.
Blessed are you who create a sacred garden
within through
times spent in silence communing with
the Friend.
Blessed are you who cultivate your heart-soil
with prayer and kind actions.
For your contemplation will become blessing;
you will radiate peace and beauty as
you live and work in the world.
You will become a mirror reflecting the light
and love of the Beloved
to all you meet.

$\mathcal{A}$waken, O friends!
Radiate the light you are!
    Do not let fear keep you from
        the truth of your being,
    nor illusions veil the innate
        beauty of your soul.
Awaken! Know that you are a holy chalice
      of light and love, for
    the Divine Guest dwells within you.
You are the holy temple of the Beloved;
    "You are the light of the world!"
        SHINE!

$\mathcal{H}$alf of the profits from these song meditations will be donated to Friends of Silence, a nonprofit endeavor to facilitate others in reverencing Silence, prayer, and contemplation and to encourage the life-giving empowerment that derives from the Silence.

For further information, write to:

FRIENDS OF SILENCE
129 Skunk Hollow Road
Jericho, Vermont 05465

Also published by Continuum

Psalms for Praying
AN INVITATION TO WHOLENESS

NAN C. MERRILL

"A much-needed resource for home liturgies and individual prayer." —*Contemporary Spirituality*

"Merrill has reworked the Book of Psalms in a loving, contemplative manner, which betrays none of the book's original vigor or essence. Rather, in a mode that is fresh and eloquent, Merrill's psalms evoke that deep sense of reverence and soul-stirring dialogue with the divine that is often eclipsed by the fear of divine wrath in the original. Highly recommended for all libraries." —*Library Journal*

"The very liveliness of the Psalms causes us to want to say them in our own language. Nan Merrill has done this marvelously, and I'm grateful for this labor of love." —Madeleine L'Engle

At your bookstore or from
The Continuum Publishing Company
370 Lexington Avenue, New York, NY 10017

www.continuum-books.com